Songs of

James Hartnell has written magazine articles, newspaper columns, sports reports, and poetry and short stories published in the UK and the USA. He has edited magazines ranging from language teaching to fishing, and is editor of *Current Accounts*, the international magazine of Bank Street Writers. James is also a contributor to Worktown Words, the writing arm of Bolton's community project Live from Worktown. He founded the Bolton International Writing Project, which saw work in twenty-nine languages published and read at various venues in nineteen shows, engaging more than five hundred immigrants from the Bolton community. He also taught English to two classes of immigrants for five years and mentored ESOL student teachers from Bolton University. With his wife and dog, James recently moved to Cheshire, where he continues to write, edit, and be involved in community projects.

"Submission? Nothing submissive about this collection – it's an acute commentary on the present state of the world. James Hartnell has always had a sharp eye for the landscape of nature, love and the absurdities of life. It's an intelligent eye, not just a maker of memorable images, but one that remembers it's an outgrowth of the brain, and can think and reflect. This is a collection to savour."

—Rod Riesco

"This collection reflects an appreciative view of a life well lived. It draws on a range of classical and contemporary sources but much of it is a paean to the beauty of small things, to the value of pausing and observing, to an appreciation of all the senses. Hartnell picks his words with care, but without employing any cheap triggers makes it clear that we often waste the best of what we have. At best we ignore it, at worst we destroy it. This collection hums with a quiet energy that repeatedly draws us back to the reality that we're here for a brief journey. We really need to savour the moment and we have a duty to make sure others can savour theirs."

—Dave Morgan

"These skilfully crafted poems, that utilise a range of sources, are a celebration of the everyday. They also embrace human difference, from Giacomo to a reclusive childhood friend. Hartnell balances nature poems, rooted in specific places and rich in arresting imagery, with ones that directly address wider themes. He explores feelings of submission and acceptance, but more sombre reflections are lifted by a pervasive tenderness and compassion."

—Helen Kay

"*Songs of Submission* exalts life in a trillion hues. It reels from the sandy test-beds of experimental Dutch flower-growing to birds tousled in the billowing air; from the fantastic fish counters of Orleans to the upper circles of Hell. It is an elegant, funny, lyrical collection in which all things play a part, both significantly and insignificantly."

—Harvey Vasey

"James has drawn on his many years as a writer to produce this wonderfully eclectic collection. His love and mastery of language is evident in every poem. Themes are nature, the joys of life and also the sadnesses and injustices of life. James has the gift of being able to move from the ordinary to something profound – 'Breakfast' being a great example of this. Some of the poems will make you smile ("the other day you found me a family of four riding the thermals several steeples high"); others will sadden ("except there's no charity shop for unwanted folk"). All will make you ponder and all you will enjoy!"

—Kathryn Brown

"This book is a superb collection of poems by a writer in his prime. There are elements of passion, anger and humour. The author isn't afraid of taking us into new realms and uses different techniques which fit in perfectly with the subject matter. It is a book to be read again and again, giving rewards and new insights every time. Buy this book – you won't regret it."

—Paul Blackburn

JAMES HARTNELL
SONGS *of* SUBMISSION

Flapjack Press
flapjackpress.co.uk

Exploring the synergy between performance and the page

Published in 2022 by Flapjack Press
Salford, Gtr Manchester
⊕ flapjackpress.co.uk f Flapjack Press
🐦 FlapjackPress ▶ Flapjack Press

ISBN 978-1-8384703-8-8

Cover photo by Rachel Loughman on Unsplash
⊕ unsplash.com/@rachelloughman

Printed by Imprint Digital
Exeter, Devon
⊕ digital.imprint.co.uk

FSC

A UNESCO City
of Literature

For Susie.

Thanks to all those poets in Write Out Loud, Bank Street
Writers, Worktown Words, and Poetry Whitchurch who have
inspired and encouraged me, to my reviewers for their kind and
thoughtful remarks, to Melanie for such a glowing Foreword and
to Paul at Flapjack Press for his excellent support and advice.

Contents

'Leopardi' was first published in *Worktown Words* [Live from Worktown]; 'The Master' was first published in the *BGS Annual;* 'Normafa' was first published in *Strategic Fit* [Wilderswood Press]; 'Back in Touch' was first published in *Worktown Words* [Live from Worktown]; 'Legacy' was first published in *Current Accounts* [Bank Street Writers]; 'Heron' was first published in *Live from Worktown Anthology 3* [Live from Worktown]; 'Doty's Mackerel' was first published in *Waiting for the Cactus* [Wilderswood Press]; 'Moments' was first published in *The Fringe Poetry Magazine* [SeaQuake Books].

James Hartnell is a poet. Well, of course he is, I am writing the Foreword for his poetry collection. But I mean in the ancient sense of the word: in Greek it means 'to make', in Sanskrit 'to gather up'. For me this epitomises James. He is not just a maker, composer, creator, performer, songwriter, but he gathers up those around him and spirits them into his perceptive and lyrical world of words.

I remember meeting James almost two decades ago and feeling completely petrified of performing, but James was so calm, so encouraging and, well, just so refreshingly honest. Poetry was not something he *did*, but poetry was something he *was*. A communicator, a crafter, a generous supporter of others, a natural storyteller and converter of cultures. Every time I have seen or heard him since our first meeting, I have come away thinking *Ah, so this is what it is to be a poet*. A two-minute conversation with him at the bar at a poetry event has been thought-provoking, illuminating, or at the very least, enchanting.

Songs of Submission is a delight, and what is distinctive about this collection is that every time you read it you are having a different conversation with him. From the very first poem, 'Waiting For The Light', it feels almost intimate, an exchange of imagination. Ever the wordsmith, James likes to play with poetic form, almost teasing with his tempo and style. Poems like 'Puerto Del Carmen' and 'Level Crossing' have a rhythmic ebb and flow, but then 'All The Gods Turned Away' is almost tsunamic. 'You Smile When You're Asleep' feels as if James is singing you a lullaby, then there's the emotional torrent of 'I Am Silence'. I find myself guided by his 'Comet' into midnight's indigo sky. I smile at his 'Smile' until I am left wanting more with his 'Last Breath'.

James Hartnell is a poet. This is not what he does, this is just who he is. These are not simply songs of submission, they are beautiful songs to submit to.

Melanie Neads
Playwright & Poet
February 2022

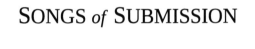

SONGS *of* SUBMISSION

We're walking with our lamps
mine on my head and yours
round your neck
while most are still asleep
an early car whispers along the main road
the nurse off up to Chester
for the day shift
then coming the other way
the first of the rumbling milk tankers
no other traffic
and we cross over and stroll
down the lane until the last
of the houses the metal gate
the meadow but it's still frozen
night at six thirty too dark
to go our separate ways
so we wait beside the gate
just a few minutes
till the blackness melts and the dawn
slides in like a latecomer
and opens the sky and I can
make out the far hedge and the next gate
our lamps are off now
and you're away hurtling through
the smoky half-light swerving
off on a huge arc and by the time
I've crossed the meadow this
daily miracle has been and gone
we're no longer waiting for the light
and I wish it were all as dependable as this
I wish.

Breakfast

For some it has to be a boiled egg
for others, two.
The suicidal like to risk it all
on a full English whilst others
cannot live without a Tesco croissant
fresh from the freezer
microwaved into crumbling flakes.
The Dutch like sprinkles in sandwiches
and slices of cheese
and the French have been dunking
their tartines for centuries.

But while we agonise over
white or brown toast
and jam or honey or marmalade
before we tuck in
those whose breakfast is chemical
wait to see if the legs will move today
others on the ventilators
have their hands held
and others take their last sip of water.

This is the seat
the seat by the path
the path alongside
the Weaver in Nantwich.
A seat set in shade.
Opposite the seat
across the river
there is an embankment
but the railway line hides away
so when a train comes through
it is gliding
on grass.
Beyond the line
a field then trees
and above the trees crows
flap and wheel
and above the crows
clouds under blue
and contrails of
planes heading south from Liverpool.
All this from the one seat.
Another day
someone else in the one seat
the view changes
the path and greetings from strangers
the river with swans and cygnets
the obvious railway line
some trees
some birds
a sky.

Giacomo sits in the family library
locked in each day till he's twenty-one
and when he emerges, a world authority
on astronomy, philology
and all the other ologies
this multilingual philosopher-poet
can't stand up straight.
He's studied too hard, his eyesight
is feeble, his back is bent
his massive intellect crushed
by the view from the window:
his favourite hill topped by
the hedgerow that robs him
of the horizon.
And the wind blows in
from that pure infinity beyond
the gardens, the slope and the hedge
and he dreams each night of
life on the other side
and plots his escape to Rome.

We had to go out further:
why were some up to their waist
others in full view?
The warning sign in the car park
was not for the likes of us.

We had to go out further:
now some of them were encrusted
– barnacles, sea grass, weed.

Just a little further:
I would be the walrus.

Then we were sinking
feet bound in black treacherous gloop
feeling the pull of that other deadly
gravity, until our knees were black
and life hesitated.

We pulled ourselves out somehow
our Saturday clothes ruined
by the foul mire.

Twice in retreat we sank again
while the Gormley men scanned the horizon
awaiting others too weak to resist.

You always spot him before me and it's you
who sometimes sees others that wheel in behind him
while I'm just stood under my empty sky
thinking about the wind that swirls up the street
it is a strong wind today that sweeps the crows
past they can't fight it and then you tell me
he's lower than usual and he's being mobbed but
the wind's so strong they can't get to him
then in he comes much closer to us
in acknowledgement see the mottled breast
as he loops for us as I fumble for a photo
but he's so quick he sheers off

chinks

climbs

gone.

The other day you found for me a family of four
riding the thermals several steeples high
two clockwise two anticlockwise but
as soon as I'd glimpsed their world
they climbed fast and were gone.

Ashley and Averill and Barnett and Beckwith
and Berrill and Daley and Deans and Edwards
and Edwards and Elks and Finucane and Flynn
and Foxon and Hesford and Hughes and Huxtable
and Jenkins and Jolly and Munro and Pitman
and Smith and Snaddon and Stewart and Stott
and Strudwick and Thomas and Tilley and Townsend
and Trepenaitis known as Trett and Twyford
and Walters and Watt and Webb and Wilson
and Woodward and Wyllie and York.

Thirty-nine that I know of
and maybe twice as many more.

They came from all over our country
and their leaders' stirring words
led every single one of them to
death in the mud
before their sixteenth birthday
death in the mud
while their generals discussed cavalry tactics
death in the mud
line after line after line of them
death in the mud
our country's most disgraceful time
death in the mud
tell your children tell their children
death in the mud
this was not glory
death in the mud

this calculated obliteration
death in the mud
this erasing of a generation
death in the mud.

And ever since that obscene slosh
of gore and mire coated the fields
death in the mud
since the trenches pooled red and brown
death in the mud
since all the Gods turned away and wept
death in the mud.

Since then, what?

Puerto Del Carmen

for Maica

Fifty-seven padlocks of love
on the chains of the little promontory
where the stray black cat sleeps on his private rock
across the way from the Gondola whose tables are being laid
for the late afternoon trade of which there is none today
and the Specials Board is signed *All with Love!!*
and the T-bone listed as *XXL.*

Behind the white-fronted sweep of the bay
the hills' outline cuts into the sky
whilst waves continue questioning the shoreline
as the sun holds off the wind
and pushes the afternoon
into a slow dance of glittering water.

The days were not empty
time wasn't short
thoughts still flashed fertile
through me
but the words ran away.

At first it was just a week
I waited unhurried for
an image to drape itself
over half a line, some willing sound
to dance across the letters
some perfume to distil
itself from the page
but the words ran away.

The weeks piled up in the corner
soon a grey mosaic of months;
I thought of these winter trees
whose leaves had sailed before
the wind and I felt just as
naked and ugly and bleak
and flattened damp underfoot.

But the year turned
deep in the frost
the days stretched a little
I started to hear them
just letters at first, then syllables
looking for a home
then big fat glorious words
bouncing and swirling around me
as I reached for my pen.

The Master

in memory of John Pilbeam

Five thousand test-tube babies grown for grading
await attention rustling lush as limes:
the offspring of the best, breathing deep the channel wind
that cools the conquered fields of Sussex chalk.

The weathered face anticipates each wind change
the seasoned eye discerning, aquiline
impatient for the rogue falling off the palette's edge
the Master at his leisure counts his leaves.

These gladiolus seedlings are his children
each labelled, each cross-referenced in his books:
the mother listed first, then the fathers one by one
meticulous defender of the cross.

In plastic tunnels, early flowers are coerced
to satisfy the seed production line:
with sable hair and patience he lifts life across the bench
and coats the sticky stigma of his choice.

The pollen grain accepted, soon the flower fades
it withers in the heat and shrivels brown
the pod that's left cocoons all the Master's godly guile:
a honeycomb of seeds some hundred strong.

Come August, as the seedling beds are flowered
a multi-coloured wash of acolytes
the Master ruthless knows very few of them will match
expectation of a very stringent kind.

Rare mavericks, unscathed, stand proud exemplars
of singular exception, breakthrough form:
the deep recessive gene tiptoes coyly into life
the Master smiles and nods into the sun.

Exhausted by the rhythm of these warm days
the Master slows and holds the gate at dusk:
leaning on his eightieth year, he recalls those shining times
when his finest clothed the polders of the Dutch.

Fond curator of these lengthy, complex bloodlines
the guardian of these cherished spikes must rest.
The Master climbs his stairs, humming faintly out of tune
and counts a million hybrids in his sleep.

The rich as always breathe
the cleanest air up here where the sky
smiles on oaks and elms
greening Schwab Hill
as far as the finest walking boots
can take you.

Sylvan shrines to wayfarer
saints, lovers on benches
along blue-chicoried tracks
recently liberated angels
fending off imaginary danger
in the country park
where the old man hires out his crates
of toys to the poorer
families up here on the bus
for a few Sunday hours closer to Heaven

drably dressed, pushing their
second-hand pushchairs, taking in
the haze of the Danube far below:
a city forever recovering, a steady
optimism undampened even by
pools of sorrow down on Andrassy.

Pelotons of cyclists spin past
the electric gates of Hotel Normafa
ten buses an hour ferry faces
up and down these soaring hills
until the sun peels away, dusk
lopes in like a bad dog

crossing the bridges that stitch
this city together.
Light bleeds fast
down these huge boulevards
but the ornate facades of Pest no longer
fear the night.

As taxis weave their diesel webs
over the river up into Buda
the road gets steeper
the granite less staunch
until the lights below are
glitter on a dressing room floor
until the chic chalet-mansions of
Normafa serrate the hill's edge.

Silence, balm: the stars kiss
the forest as it closes its last flowers
for another night while down by the river
a million tenants in '60s tenements
dare to dream the democratic dream.

On the still Sunday road
it's just gone seven.
Three happy cyclists greet me
as they fizz past.
I'm walking the dog
and I press on. Uneventful.
But on the way back
I see her, unrecognisable at first.
Just a brown lump on the tarmac.
There's very little traffic.
I get a puzzled dog home quickly
and go back to her.
She is peaceful
still
long gone.
I pick her up, stroke the mottled chest
the perfectly arranged wing feathers
willing her to burst back into her young life
and fly off. If only.
I bring her home, take the spade
across the field to the old oak.
Now she can rest in the shade
away from men and machines.
Back home I realise I've forgotten
how hot tears are
as I cry quietly into my coffee.

Her resistance was low in the stationery room where she lingered amongst the supplies, tried to lean into a fresh stack of reams of 80grams but it was no good. She deserved better, longed for the joy of hand-made, of very special quality, of true craftsmanship, not mere bank and bond.

After work, in the second-hand book shop, she trembled and groaned quietly as she got that sensual fix she had been after all day, as the lignin in the cheap paperbacks slid into her airways and caressed her being. An hour later, the art shop next door was closed. She cursed – no rough cartridge tonight. She hurried home, knowing that evening awaited with the tastes, smells, and textures that would surely fulfil her longing.

But the routine first: the door closed, the hall table, the size-free blotter, aperitif for the sensations to come. In the drawing room, her precious Victorian collection in drawer after drawer, alum-based, slow-fire letters, postcards, yellowing deliciously down the years, no bleach, no sulphate, no modern deception, and she caressed and stroked them and smelt their fidelity. Her treasures, her very private secrets never shared.

She had brought in from the hall a new packet from her specialist in the States which she now considered with a particular fond but measured anticipation. For five minutes she turned it in her hands, held it, smelt it, savoured an exact aroma which she identified with a half-smile as Tyvek, the latest synthetic, an ironic, witty choice. She passed the next half hour enjoying the wrapper, a first incision in one perfectly taped corner, then a wonderful slow ritual of unwrapping, unfolding, uncreasing, smoothing and stroking the Tyvek.

Breathless, she stood up and moved away; it was too soon. In the kitchen she dined simply and happily, the coating of the

Vietnamese nems melting gradually in her mouth. Licking her lips, she returned to the dining room, her pulse quickening. She slid the wrapper carefully to one side and caught her breath as the contents were fully exposed to her, perfect, hand-made sheets that made her first gasp then sigh loudly as she discovered aspect after aspect of the skill, love, devotion expended on this epitome of the craft.

She broke away from them. The records! She must do the entries properly in her bespoke ledger: no shabby Moleskine tat, hers was a gilt-embossed, calf-bound, gold padlocked unique work of art. She wrote steadily, filling her columns with love.

And then she was free at last to hold and fondle her delight, to run her finger oh so slowly down the deckle edge, to stroke the cross grain, to inhale the essence of the sheets, as the euphoria engulfed her as she knew it would, and her head fell back as she was romanced, enthralled and defined by her secret love.

He was never right
not like the rest of us
though he lived in the same street.
He'd play sometimes
but nothing rough
and never too far
from his front door.
The rest of us
we'd be off down the park
before our Mum could
look at the clock
but he'd never come
always had some excuse
always something
or just an
'I don't think so – not today'.
Maybe it was his glasses
those thick black frames
or that jibby bottom lip
he got from his Dad…
We quarrelled once
over a Dinky
and the fact that he always
beat everybody at chess so there
and he threw his toy rifle
(with a real tin barrel)
threw it at me
and the circular
scar's still here on my knee.
I limped home bravely
howling indoors

I'd never walk again
it was definitely broken
my knee was broken for life
or at least until I was nine
in five days' time.
He was never right
but he never deserved
all those breakdowns
and all those years
on his own in hospital.
I think he knew all along
what was coming
right from the time
he threw the rifle
knew that he wasn't
like the rest of us
though he lived in the same street.

As you sit in your carriage with your thoughts
and plans and regrets and your bad decisions
which you tell yourself are better than no decision
the houses and gardens and streets and fields
watch you slip past unmoved by your worries
and withheld tears while you ignore them all
just as you ignore all these people on their phones
just as you've been discarding them like worn out clothes
except there's no charity shop for unwanted folk.

You would like to destroy the WiFi, shut down every site
turn all these phones into flowers.
The surprise on their faces as they looked for a keypad
in the middle of a rose or tried speaking into a tulip!
For the first time ever, you'd watch passengers
looking at each other too traumatised to speak
dreading this new intimacy.
Because without phones
they would have nothing to say.

The scrag end of March:
sunshine and a cold wind which runs
that seam between winter and summer
which was once spring.

Most trees are sad
hoping for a new dress.
The empty sky closes off
the distant horizon, as unreachable
as a rainbow. It hurts that you never
get to hold it close, breathe it in.

A surly north-easterly rakes
the surface a while then relents.
The boats snooze at their moorings
huddled along the bank
stoked up, locked down.

Come April, traffic increases
boats climb the staircase.
I can at last sit and concentrate hard
on my gongoozling
that dying art of watching
time unfold over water.

Feeling down? Ashamed? Disappointed in yourself?
Let's take a little guided fantasy to Dante's *Inferno*.
You might find yourself with me
in the higher circles of Hell
lightly punished for Lust, Gluttony, Greed.
Yes, I'll be there! And I'll have more than
a short stay further down in Circle Six
with all the other heretics.

But if you look way, way down
past Circle Seven with all the violent herd
and, what seems really unfair, all the suicides
even further down, just peer into the dark void
where you and I won't be going:
you can't see much at all
but you can hear the sad screams and wailing
smell the burning, bubbling tar, feel the endless agony.

Circle Eight is a horrendous place
a place of stark, naked dread.
It's the only one with ten trenches of filth and unbearable pain
reserved exclusively for corrupt politicians
hypocrites, liars and their ilk.

There. Deep breath.
Up you come.
And open your eyes.
You're feeling better already.

Level Crossing

Amber, red times three
the gates come down
left side first, then the right.
It's a long wait
but no one breaks the rules.
Civil, polite, silent.
To my left a pedestrian
on crutches and another
with a playful dog.
A young man strides up over
the footbridge. He has
no doubt waited before.

We sit while the three red
lights flash. I realise
this is where we are.
Five minutes pass.
I'm expecting a long line
of trucks, maybe two locos.
Nothing is certain.
The air horn's two-tone salute:
just one lonely unit trundles through.
Life is still on hold
even when the gates lift
and our engines start.

We drive off together:
a convoy through
the echo of waiting.

Back in touch with friends from half a century ago
I learn that others have gone or are all but gone from disease
and I ponder which news saddens me more.
I can accept inevitable loss but the tragic enfeeblement
of the wonderful minds of those I loved rips deep into me.
And I am more than fortunate, having come close to death myself.
There is no equation: the way I lived compared to
their orderly, healthy, single-partnered lifestyle
turns logic inside out as I thrive while they get
struck down, crumble and grimace.
Ever since my teens, every decade has seen
more than one friend lost to suicide
or just plain bad luck. Maybe we've all known this.
At least with a death you can do nothing but remember and mourn.
With disease, the thwarting of future happiness
and the brick wall of a worsening condition
conspire to shatter your dream of rekindling a former friendship.
Back in touch with friends, you can sign off all your texts with love
and really mean it.

Spun out strung out helices of whispering
instincts deep within the murmuring of hidden generations
long before writing led us into misinterpretation
enslaving tales, stifling our inklings of this indifferent harmony
there was a way through the mist and some knew
and they felt the signs even then
whilst others laughed and stayed by the river
or on the mountain and drowned or froze to death.
Those of us who loved the mist
wooed the right gods, we heard our forefathers
deep within we knew there was no fighting it
the heavens turned, the moon soared across the sky and
the voices of spirits guided us through
the tangle of our brief years until we too became whispers
of comfort for those who would listen.

You stand just across the lane and tower over the view.
Behind you, a roll of fields and trees that bubble across the skyline
and you've seen it all and know more than most.

Let's say 200 years?
So you arrived just after Waterloo and ever since
just carnage and wars
each more appalling than the last
and you have stood while millions have fallen.

Pain seeps through your bark. I can smell your disgust at men.
You are more stoical than any of us though some nights
I think I hear you weep on the wind.

Comet

for Chris Woods

Where the high horizon sutures the sky
to Holcombe Moor
way up above the padlocked hut
his dog tailwags up ahead alongside the one
stringvested hillrunner
while he and his alchemist hold
this season-soaked day about them
as they calibrate and calculate
and examine a sclerotic sky for
one sign of it.

But jagged time arcs away
towards Two Brooks and beyond
as the weather presents
a fond bleakness.

Down the generations
it's a night tingling with stars
that grants his last wish to his grandchildren
now full-grown who step aside for
the ghost of the hillrunner
as they screen subatomic
pointing the autoscope
to capture at last
the faithful messenger sizzling
through an ocean of sky.

Maybe the words sing more clearly written on Lokta
but it's all out of tune today: no view from the bridge
the far shore gone.

Time spins, slowing then keeling over like
a child's top, the sun's warmth stolen
by a knifing wind that seethes, swirls across the water
pushing onward foreign rumours, sizzling code flakes
mile-high text stacks, a million voices
arcing and crackling off the Winter Hill mast.

Briefly irked by this cyberstorm
my avian therapist ghosts her way up the brook
gliding to Zen through the data stream.

Zeno:

The morbid undertones to these sunny days, to these nights
where black is bleak remind us our time is broken.
Doubt, despair, deception, denial. No one brave enough to voice it.
But just think. You lived your best days long ago.
Science has wept. The dead as always outnumber the living.
Money was just a concept and the Vaccine Wars are over.
We have had our last briefing.

Pilgrim:

And yet I have seen good. On my way here
I met with true altruism, faith, hope and love.
We who remain may be few but we are one in our determination.

Zeno:

It is too late. Accept this.

Pilgrim:

That I cannot. Our orphans need us. I have no family left
but I can still turn up and keep others alive.

Zeno:

There is no place here for impulse or emotion. We are not animals.

Pilgrim:

Caring is the bravest of acts in these times. I will not walk away.

Zeno:

You are mistaken. The end begins here.

Pilgrim:

I was conceived in love and hope. These have served me well
and are reliable companions.

Zeno:

As always, your faith is misplaced.
Just as the herd chose to follow greedy autocrats to their doom
and died with lies and broken promises as their testament
so your emotion and empathy will lead to suffering
as your values are shipwrecked by a fickle mob.
Nothing has any lasting value.

Pilgrim:

It is empathy not apathy that will redeem us.

Zeno:

Did the mob show empathy when they wrecked
every Town Hall in the country? No. Thus will it be.

Pilgrim:

You know full well the people were left to starve while the officials
were well fed and protected by the Homeless Secretary.

Zeno:

Do not let your emotions cloud the issue.
The masses deserve nothing.

Pilgrim:

We are born and die. It is how we live and love that defines us.
Each of us in need deserves what others can provide.

You smile when you're asleep
and wake and turn beside me.
You roll into my flank
and watch our hands entwine.
You soften as we kiss
and stir as I caress you.
You pull me with your hands
and lock your eyes on mine.
You shake as love attends
enfolded in my being.
You stroke my shoulder soothing
and trace a lover's line.

The veil for your embarrassment
the chokehold of collusion
the stifling of your secret sin
the padlock to your lonely heart
these arms that pin you down

and yes I am your friend and saviour
a truce in your battle with the world
your survival space till morning

so you hate me so you love me
and the hours churn on
and no noise can smother me

I am so sweet
like your last goodbye
relentlessly painful
like the hurt you will cause
implacable eternal
like the stars beyond forever.

The Stop 'n' Shop in Orleans
displays its mackerel
as perfectly the same as

they've always been
yet folk seem to approach
this counter from the shellfish end

or the middle where the salmon
glitter, somehow avoiding the left
end without knowing why

just pointing towards it when
they want mackerel as if that end's
off-limits, an altar or a work of art

revered. The cognoscenti only
buy on certain days, aware
of how the gleam can

fade, the blood-rimmed eye
tire under the lights, weary of
the stares of bargain hunters

chasing reductions, counting
their toes. Just once, a poet
held this hallowed ground

stood where no one ever stands
hushed by these black-barred
clones. Someone called security

though nobody knew who.
But everybody said you just
don't stare at fish for an hour

unless you're an accomplice
a unibomber's mate or a
look-out for a mass heist

about to hit 24 checkouts
simultaneously. No,
fishwatching is a dead giveaway

it shows you have a real
problem with the world view
of mackerel. As store guards

shouted he moved away
from the counter; as
they aimed their guns

he drew a pen from his
inside pocket, smiling
oblivious.

On the back of an
old envelope he wrote the words
he had been waiting for

all summer, words that
captured oil on water
that exalted a uniformity.

That week I dreamed of the weirdest of beasts
pursued one night by polar bears
then hellish hounds all hoary with ice
then Grendel's claw coming toward me
whichever way I chose to look.
Another night a new terror
as squalid scaly monsters threw me
to and fro like a toy for their pleasure
till I was bruised and broken and battered and pulped.
Worst was the way the steel failed
after the earth-dragon's fangs had sunk into me.
How many heroes had hacked out their glory
wielding this blade that had always won through?
Fate goes ever as fate must.
Modern warriors fight modern wars
but the best sleep badly and believe in dragons.

Going back or looking ahead
you're squandering the joy of now
you're trailblazing another path
into memory, revisiting places
evoking people but they're just
shells. You reorganise
the past so many times to suit
yourself. You so want to hold
on to now but this present
with its infinite deck
deals you a new card even as
you're trying to look at the one
in your hand. Young and bulletproof
with twenty thousand days ahead
nothing seemed to matter. Now
with who knows how many
hours left, with the unsaid goodbyes
haunting you, it's time.
Time to delight in the remaining
half a million moments, each one
glittering and exquisite.

They give me the top chair
testbed for commentary
on all things erudite
or in my case dartboard
with a blonde on either side
and the path to tread
between politesse
and controversy
is a fine wine line
watch your ass
shield your glass
flatter where it matters
and heed the preprandial warnings
to keep it light
as these people count
so I try.

The Professor of Applied Neuromancy
who seems impervious to alcohol
hits me with nurture versus nature
and I go for broke
and get lucky as he bellows agreement
but I blunder
when his wife refers to her MSc and bar
as the key to getting on
and I mishear and say
that it's just a matter of getting
any old crap in the right order
for her editor because
he's a bigoted tart
who wouldn't know
a good writer from a horse

and the next morning
the other blonde
reminds me that I may have
burnt my gondolas
around the nth bottle of Chianti.

Somewhere between saffron and terracotta
but south of tangerine the patchouli of a smile
slips soft into this slowing evening
folds into a harmony of
synaptic electric blue
and Dorian aquamarine
lifts the last hours of the day
out of the dove and the slate and the jet
up into amethyst cobalt
delphinium cornflower
the warmer blues of connection.

Reflections of barley lampshades
khaki-washed Rodins float on
midnight indigo outside the
panoramic window whilst inside
champagne shadows blur into
the lamplight mute the knifed angles
the harsh ivory cornices
the razor-edged leaves of a plant
that hears everything in emerald
and the smile shimmers
reverberates golden through the night.

Up there in the ether
the talk is of chromosomes
n-counts, ploidy and pollen banks.
Planting is in the thousands
for a selection of one or none.
I've met some of the Gods
of phytogenetics and worshipped
in their fields.

Amateurs aim at beauty and colour
but the pros aim for the market.
They know what will sell and
they breed new plants to suit.
In Holland I have dreamed
in the sandy testbeds
and marvelled at the beauty of
the also-rans, the rejects that
get thrown away by the thousand.
I have seen the most amazing
breakthroughs, huge achievements
that took my breath away
which the public will never see
for crazy commercial reasons.

The breeders examine their stock
and come in
covered in pollen
like golden Greek gods
with a Tupperwared lunch.

At perfect temperatures
they spend hours
crossing and bagging and labelling
with an eight-digit number
entering it all in the family album
with photos of parents
and grandparents
and aunts and uncles
and brothers and sisters
and dates and more dates
a meticulous obsession.

In the supermarkets
the buyer might try
one new line per year at the most.
Price is everything.

It is Sunday
in early May:
always seems so clear and clean
these fresh soft days of birds in gardens
a distant mower, the low cloud holds
us in on an unremarkable estate
as we wait.

We have a big plan
a double migration
from town to village to village:
the roof is on, we'll soon be in.
I'm so glad my best friend
brought me
to a better place.

The birds continue
the mower has stopped
the grass grows
the dog barks at ghosts in the street
then it's all still again:
in early May
it is Sunday.

Before breakfast we are on a platform
on the cliffside overlooking the Aegean
receiving celestial energy.

I've hauled down the sun and the moon
touched grass, flown my dragon
and downed my dog.

I have flowed from Tadasana
to Shavasana, from Krishna
to Karate Kid.

With stability before mobility
I am Warrior One and Two
before transforming from
Sphinx to Cobra to Golden Eagle.

Then relax...

As the final filigree of thoughts
wafts out of my meditation
the teacher says calmly
'Make this your last breath.'